SACRAMENTO PUBLIC LIBRARY

D0099969

5814

1/2011

SCARY STORIES

BONE-CHILLING
MYTHS

By Tim O'Shei

Consultant:
Simon J. Bronner, PhD
Distinguished Professor of American Studies and Folklore
Fellow, American Folklore Society
The Pennsylvania State University, Harrisburg

CAPSTONE PRESS
a capstone imprint

Edge Books are published by Capstone Press,
151 Good Counsel Drive, P.O. Box 669, Mankato, Minnesota 56002.
www.capstonepub.com

Copyright © 2011 by Capstone Press, a Capstone imprint.
All rights reserved.
No part of this publication may be reproduced in whole or in part,
or stored in a retrieval system, or transmitted in any form or by any means, electronic,
mechanical, photocopying, recording, or otherwise, without
written permission of the publisher.
For information regarding permission, write to Capstone Press,
151 Good Counsel Drive, P.O. Box 669, Dept. R, Mankato, Minnesota 56002.

Printed in the United States of America in Stevens Point, Wisconsin.
102010
005977R

Books published by Capstone Press are manufactured with paper
containing at least 10 percent post-consumer waste.

Library of Congress Cataloging-in-Publication Data
O'Shei, Tim.
  Bone-chilling myths / by Tim O'Shei.
    p. cm.—(Edge books. Scary stories)
  Summary: "Describes scary myths, including Heracles and the Hydra
and Marduk and Tiamat"—Provided by publisher.
  Includes bibliographical references and index.
  ISBN 978-1-4296-4573-7 (library binding)
  1. Mythology—Juvenile literature. I. Title. II. Series.
  BL312.O84 2011
  398'.4—dc22   2010001356

Editorial Credits

Megan Peterson, editor; Ted Williams, designer; Kelly Garvin, media researcher;
    Laura Manthe, production specialist

Photo Credits

Alamy/The Print Collector, 4

The Bridgeman Art Library International/British Museum, London, UK, 16;
    Giraudon/Musee des Beaux-Arts, Orleans, France, 7

Capstone Studio/Karon Dubke, scaremeter, 29

Dreamstime/Courtney Lanier, 22; Omidii, 10

Getty Images/Dorling Kindersley, 19; Hulton Archive, 25

Mary Evans Picture Library, 15, 26; Grenville Collins Postcard Collection, 9

Shutterstock/Michael Lynch, 20; Robert King, 12; Vladimir Wrangel, cover

Design Elements

Shutterstock/averole (hand prints), Charles Taylor (rusty background), David M.
    Schrader (paper w/tape), DCD (dribbles), Eugene Ivanov (border), George
    Nazmi Bebawi (fly), Gordan (borders), Hal_P (fingerprints), hfng (word
    bubble), Ian O'Ha (spider web), Kirsty Pargeter (brush strokes border),
    oxygen64 (frames), Ralf Juergen Kraft (computer bug), silver-john (paper),
    Subbotina Anna (fly), Thomas Bethge (tapes), xjbxjhxm123 (button)

TABLE OF CONTENTS

According to Norse myths, the god Thor created lightning when he threw his hammer.

A CURIOUS STORY

"Why?" That single word might be the world's most common question. People are curious. They want to know why and how certain events happen.

Long ago, people used myths, or stories, to explain how humans and Earth were created. People also told myths about things like wind and lightning. The Norse god Thor threw his hammer to create lightning. The Chinese god Fei Lian carried the wind in a bag. Myths even helped explain bad things like sickness and death. In a Greek myth, evil spread to the world when Pandora, the first woman, opened a jar.

Every **culture** has its own myths. Many myths began in ancient times as word-of-mouth stories. These stories were eventually recorded. Around 700 BC, Homer wrote about many Greek gods in his poems the *Iliad* and the *Odyssey*.

Not all myths are scary. But from deadly dragons to a creepy underworld, the myths you'll find here are downright terrifying. Read with the lights on!

culture—a people's way of life, ideas, customs, and traditions

A ROCK-HARD LESSON
A GREEK MYTH

SCARY

Apollo, the god of archery, pulled an arrow from his **quiver**. He set it in his bow. Quietly he pulled back the arrow, took aim, and fired.

Thwack! Apollo quickly fired six more arrows. Thwack! Splat! He killed the seven sons of Niobe, queen of the Greek city Thebes.

Apollo launched the bloody attack after Niobe bragged about her large family. Niobe believed her large family made her more important than other mothers, including Apollo's mother, Leto. Leto only had one son and one daughter—the twins Apollo and Artemis (AR-tuh-muhss).

quiver—a case for carrying or holding arrows

Leto was quiet and modest. She never bragged. But she had a temper, and Niobe's bragging made her angry. "Your sons are dead," Leto said to Niobe. "Will you apologize for bragging?"

Niobe was shocked and saddened. But she refused to apologize. "No!" she said. "I still have seven daughters."

Leto ordered her daughter, Artemis, to kill Niobe's daughters. Artemis obeyed. Like her brother, she used arrows to kill Niobe's seven daughters.

Leto found Niobe after the attack. "Now you have no children!" she said. "Will you apologize?"

Niobe didn't answer. Instead, she fled all the way to the top of a mountain called Sipylus. She was sad and couldn't stop crying. Leto's husband, the god Zeus, decided to end Niobe's sadness. He used his magical powers to turn her into rock. But even as solid stone, Niobe's tears continued.

Fear Fact

A carved figure (pictured) on Mount Sipylus in modern-day Turkey was once thought to be Niobe. Today some people associate a nearby natural rock formation with Niobe.

SAVING THE LAST SISTER

A JAPANESE MYTH

VERY SCARY

A woman stood trembling before a dragon with eight heads and eight tails. She was trapped in a shady patch of forest. The leaves on the trees were brown and crinkly, burnt by the dragon's fiery breath. The dragon's 16 red eyes stared at the woman. Drool dripped from the monster's many lips and turned to steam as it hit the forest floor. The woman had no doubt that the dragon was about to chew her to bits. It had already killed her seven older sisters.

Suddenly, a man soared overhead. He dropped from the heavens, clinging to a snake. The man wore a large, baggy cloak that flapped in the wind as he touched the ground.

The dragon's eight heads let out piercing screeches. Its scaly lips curled back to reveal rows of sharp teeth. But the man, who held no weapons, looked calm and confident. "How is he going to protect himself?" the woman wondered.

The man slowly reached inside his cloak. He pulled out eight bowls of a strong drink. The man smiled and offered them to the dragon. The monster sniffed the liquid with each of its eight noses. Then, with a happy grunt, it quickly lapped up all the liquid. The dragon's eyelids soon grew heavy, and it fell asleep.

The woman watched the man reach back into his cloak. This time he pulled out a sharp sword. In a lightning-fast swoop, he thrust the sword into the sleeping dragon's belly. The man then pushed the weapon upward, stabbing the dragon's heart.

The man inspected the dragon and found a magical sword in its tail. He pulled out the sword and then turned to the woman. "I am Susano'o, the god of thunder." The pair quickly fell in love and were married.

Fear Fact

The magical sword Susano'o pulled from the dragon's tail became a Japanese symbol of power.

WINNING THE WORLD FROM EVIL
A BABYLONIAN MYTH

VERY SCARY

Tiamat was an evil dragon with wings and a snakelike body. She wanted to rule the universe. Along with her husband, Apsu, Tiamat hatched a plan to fight the gods and destroy all she could. But a god named Ea overheard Tiamat's plan. Ea was the god of wisdom. Ea knew it wouldn't be wise to let Tiamat run wild. He killed Tiamat's husband.

Tiamat formed an army of dragons, snakes, scorpions, and other dangerous creatures. Her army held the tablets of destiny. Whoever had these tablets would rule the universe.

The gods wanted to take the tablets from Tiamat. At first, they tried a peaceful approach. The gods visited Tiamat, but her disgusting, gnarled face scared them away. Marduk, Ea's son, decided to lead the other gods in a battle against Tiamat.

Marduk rode in a chariot as he led the battle against Tiamat.

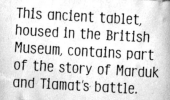

This ancient tablet, housed in the British Museum, contains part of the story of Marduk and Tiamat's battle.

Using a wide net, the gods trapped Tiamat. She threw open her massive jaws in surprise. Her mouth was many miles wide, and Marduk had an idea. He ordered the winds to swoosh into Tiamat's mouth and fill her stomach. Tiamat inflated like a balloon. Marduk then used a spear to pop her open, cut away her guts, and stab her heart.

Marduk sliced Tiamat's body in half. He used the upper part of her body to create the heavens. The lower part of her body became the floor of the ocean. Tiamat's bodily fluids became the clouds, and her eyes became rivers.

The world was formed, and the gods ruled it. They had saved the universe from the evil Tiamat.

FEAR FACT

In Babylonian myths, Tiamat is the mother of all that exists, including the gods.

CHOPPED TO BITS
A MAYAN MYTH

Freaky Scary

A severed, rotting head hung from a tree. Brothers Hunahpu (hoo-nah-POO) and Xbalanque (sha-bah-lahn-KAY) were filled with anger. The head belonged to their father, Hun.

The lords of Xibalba (shee-bahl-BAH), the underworld of the **Maya**, had killed Hun. To celebrate their victory, the lords chopped off Hun's head and displayed it on a tree branch.

The lords then challenged Hunahpu and Xbalanque to a ball game. They also said the brothers must first survive a series of dangerous challenges. Houses filled with sharp knives, hungry jaguars, and flying bats awaited the brothers in Xibalba.

Xbalanque and Hunahpu

Hunahpu and Xbalanque were eager to begin the challenges. They walked the thorn-covered road that led to Xibalba and entered the House of Knives. Row after row of razor-sharp knives filled the house. The knives sliced through the air in every direction. But the brothers stayed calm. They spoke to the knives in a soothing voice. The knives stopped thrashing.

Maya—an ancient civilization that extended through southern Mexico and Central America

Next, muscular, bloodthirsty cats snapped their teeth in the House of Jaguars. The brothers found a pile of bones. They threw the bones into the cats' mouths. While the jaguars gnawed on the bones, Hunahpu and Xbalanque escaped unharmed.

But the House of Bats proved to be a problem. The winged creatures soared in every direction. They bared their sharp fangs, ready to sink their teeth into the brothers' flesh. Hunahpu and Xbalanque found a place to hide. But Hunahpu made a mistake—he stuck his head out of his hiding place. That's when one of the bats sliced off Hunahpu's head!

Since the brothers were **divine**, Hunahpu didn't die. He escaped from the House of Bats and used a gourd for a head. The lords then started the ball game, using Hunahpu's sliced-off head for the ball. When the lords weren't looking, Xbalanque threw the gourd into the game. He then took back his brother's head.

The angry lords of Xibalba challenged the brothers to fly over fire. Instead, the brothers jumped into the flames! Screaming, they crumpled to the ground. The flames appeared to swallow them up.

The lords of Xibalba celebrated their victory. But a few days later, Hunahpu and Xbalanque returned to Xibalba. They sneaked up on the lords and chopped them into pieces. Finally, they had gotten revenge for their father's death.

divine—to do with or from God, or a god

FEAR FACT

The phoenix is a mythical bird whose life never ends. When the phoenix grows old and "dies," it is immediately reborn as a baby bird. The phoenix is seen in Egyptian and Greek myths. It even appears in the Harry Potter books and movies.

A NASTY BURN
A GREEK MYTH

Freaky Scary

A gray mist rolled over the soggy swamp. Out of the murky water slithered a snakelike creature with nine heads. When it got hungry, this monster was known to chomp on cows with its sharp fangs. Other times it feasted on humans. The Hydra was a murdering monster—and Heracles (HARE-uh-klees) was going to stop it.

Heracles was strong and quick. But killing the Hydra would not be an easy task. A single whiff of the Hydra's breath could kill. Heracles had to hold his breath while fighting.

Roar! The Hydra let out a hot, poisonous rumble. Smoky air stung Heracles' eyes. He reared back with the sword and swung it like a baseball bat.

Swish! Heracles chopped off one of the Hydra's nasty heads. Heracles relaxed his muscles just a bit. But then he heard a pair of popping sounds. His eyes bolted upward. Two new heads grew in the place of the head Heracles had cut off. Heracles swung his sword again. This time he sliced off both new heads. Pop, pop, pop, pop! Four new heads instantly grew in their places.

Heracles kept cutting off heads. And the Hydra kept growing new ones. The battle was exhausting. Heracles was barely able to hold his breath. He began to lose strength.

But then help arrived. Heracles' nephew Iolaus (eye-oh-LAY-uhss) stepped in with a flaming torch. When Heracles cut off a head, Iolaus used the flame to burn the Hydra's flesh closed. Both men cringed at the smell of the burning bones and guts. But the plan worked—no new heads appeared. Cut by cut, burn by burn, Heracles and Iolaus removed the Hydra's heads.

But the Hydra's last remaining head couldn't be removed with a sword. Would the monster escape alive?

Heracles used a club to smash the Hydra's remaining head. He then grabbed the head, twisted it, and tore it off. Heracles buried the head and put a huge boulder on top of the hole. The Hydra was finally dead. And Heracles could breathe again!

Heracles (left) and Iolaus (right) battled the deadly Hydra monster.

FEAR FACT

In ancient Greek myths, Heracles was a hero known for his great strength. While in his cradle, Heracles killed two snakes. The ancient Romans had their own version of Heracles called Hercules.

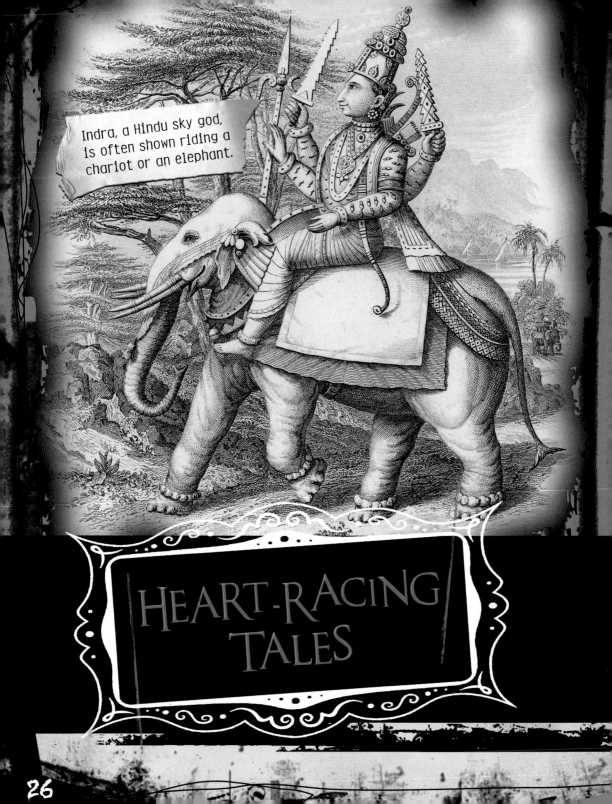

Indra, a Hindu sky god, is often shown riding a chariot or an elephant.

HEART-RACING TALES

The myths in this book have been scaring people for thousands of years. Filled with **supernatural** events, these stories may seem unbelievable. But the people who heard them long ago considered them to be true.

Myths from different cultures sometimes have similar stories and characters. The Greek god Zeus and the Hindu god Indra are sky gods. Both gods use lightning bolts for weapons. Some scholars believe that when societies broke apart, they took their myths with them. These new societies then created their own versions of the same myths. Myths were also spread as people traveled and traded goods. In some cases, different cultures simply reacted to the world in similar ways.

supernatural—something that cannot be given an ordinary explanation

PERFECT YOUR SCARY STORYTELLING

To tell a truly bone-chilling myth, start by asking, "Have you ever wondered why it's bad to brag?" Or, "Do you know why the strongest people don't always win a fight?" Next, tell where your myth comes from. Include as much detail as you can. Describe the smells and sounds of the story. Hint at who lives and who dies, but don't give away the ending.

It's okay to add or change a detail here and there. But don't change the meaning of the story. Remember, myths are supposed to teach people about the world. Now turn off the lights and make your friends' hearts race with excitement and fear!

FEAR FACT

The word "myth" comes from the Greek word *mythos*, which means a story or speech.

GLOSSARY

Babylonian (bab-uh-LOW-nyee-uhn)—of or relating to Babylonia; Babylonia was an ancient civilization in present-day central and southern Iraq that lasted from about 2000 to 500 BC

culture (KUHL-chuhr)—a people's way of life, ideas, customs, and traditions

divine (duh-VYN)—to do with or from God, or a god

Maya (MYE-uh)—an ancient civilization that extended through southern Mexico and Central America from 2000 BC until the mid-1500s

quiver (KWIV-ur)—a case for carrying or holding arrows

revenge (rih-VENJ)—an action taken to cause harm to someone for a wrong or injury they caused

supernatural (soo-pur-NACH-ur-uhl)—something that cannot be given an ordinary explanation

READ MORE

Horowitz, Anthony. *Myths and Legends.* Boston: Kingfisher, 2007.

Kopp, Megan. *Scary Folktales.* Scary Stories. Mankato, Minn.: Capstone Press, 2011.

Storrie, Paul. *Hercules: The Twelve Labors.* Graphic Myths and Legends. Minneapolis: Lerner, 2007.

Yomtov, Nel. *Theseus and the Minotaur.* Graphic Revolve. Minneapolis: Stone Arch Books, 2009.

INTERNET SITES

FactHound offers a safe, fun way to find Internet sites related to this book. All of the sites on FactHound have been researched by our staff.

Here's all you do:

Visit *www.facthound.com*

Type in this code: 9781429645737

INDEX